THE
DALAI
LAMA
BOOK OF
QUOTES

A COLLECTION OF SPEECHES,
QUOTATIONS, ESSAYS, AND
ADVICE FROM HIS HOLINESS

THE
DALAI
LAMA
BOOK OF
QUOTES

A COLLECTION OF SPEECHES, QUOTATIONS, ESSAYS, AND ADVICE FROM HIS HOLINESS

EDITED BY TRAVIS HELLSTROM

Hatherleigh Press is committed to preserving and protecting the natural resources of the earth. Environmentally responsible and sustainable practices are embraced within the company's mission statement.

Visit us at www.hatherleighpress.com and register online for free offers, discounts, special events, and more.

The Dalai Lama Book of Quotes
Text Copyright © 2016 Travis Hellstrom

Library of Congress Cataloging-in-Publication Data
is available.
ISBN: 978-1-57826-640-1

Design by Carolyn Kasper

Printed in the United States
10 9 8 7 6 5

CONTENTS

INTRODUCTION

HIS HOLINESS the XIV Dalai Lama is one of the great thinkers of our time. He has shared his wisdom with us throughout the world in speeches, interviews, stories, and dozens of books. But in seeking to learn from his wise words, where should you begin? In *The Dalai Lama Book of Quotes* we have taken some of the Dalai Lama's most loved wisdom from over 40 years of teaching and shared them in short and easy to remember quotes. The language may be simple, but we trust you will find the wisdom of His Holiness to be profound.

Whether you are reading just one quote at a time or enjoying them all in one reading, we hope the wisdom of the Dalai Lama is helpful and powerful for you, as it has been for us.

As His Holiness says, "If anything I've said seems useful to you, I'm glad. If not, don't worry. Just forget about it."

LOVE

The need for love lies at the very foundation of human existence.

If our love for someone is based largely on attraction, whether it be their looks or some other superficial characteristic, our feelings for that person are liable, over time, to evaporate. When they lose the quality we found alluring, the situation can change completely, this despite their being the same person. This is why intimate relationships based purely on attraction are almost always unstable.

If you are showing love to your fellow human beings, you are showing love to your God.

We humans have existed in our present form for about 100,000 years. I believe that if during this time the human mind had been primarily controlled by anger and hatred, our overall population would have decreased. But today, despite all our wars, we find that the human population is greater than ever. This clearly indicates to me that love and compassion predominate in the world. And this is why unpleasant events are "news"; compassionate activities are so much a part of daily life that they are taken for granted and, therefore, largely ignored.

A loving atmosphere in your home is the foundation for your life.

Harming or destroying any being from the highest to the lowest, from a human to the tiniest insect, must at all costs be avoided. The foundation of all spiritual practice is love.

Love and compassion are necessities, not luxuries. Without them humanity cannot survive.

Human affection is the foundation of proper development.

We have genuine friendship when it is based on true human feeling, a feeling of closeness in which there is a sense of sharing and connectedness. I would call this type of friendship genuine because it is not affected by the increase or decrease of the individual's wealth, status or power. The factor that sustains that friendship is whether or not the two people have mutual feelings of love and affection.

Take in account that great love and great achievements involve great risk.

To generate true love, you need to know how it differs from attachment.

Unfortunately, love and compassion have been omitted from too many spheres of social interaction for too long. Usually confined to family and home, their practice in public life is considered impractical, even naive. This is tragic.

Love for others and respect for their rights and dignity, no matter who or what they are: ultimately these are all we need. So long as we practice these in our daily lives, then no matter if we are learned or unlearned, whether we believe in Buddha or God, or follow some other religion or none at all, as long as we have compassion for others and conduct ourselves with restraint out of a sense of responsibility, there is no doubt we will be happy.

Along with love, compassion is the face of altruism. It is a feeling from deep in the heart that you cannot bear others' suffering without acting to relieve it.

With love that is simply attachment, the slightest change in the object, such as a tiny change of attitude, immediately causes you to change. This is because your emotion is based on something very superficial. Take, for example, a new marriage. Often after a few weeks, months, or years the couple becomes enemies and finish up getting divorced. They married deeply in love—nobody marries with hatred—but after a short time everything changed. Why?

The best relationship is one in which your love for each other exceeds your need for each other.

If a person has never encountered love toward himself or herself from any quarter, it is a very sad thing. But if that person can meet even one person who will show unconditional love—simply acceptance and compassion—if he knows that he is an object of someone else's affection and love, it is bound to have an impact, and this will be appreciated. Because there is a seed in himself, this act of love will start to catalyze or ripen that seed.

If you do not have the capacity to love yourself, then there is simply no basis on which to build a sense of caring toward others.

There are different types of attachment in relation to different objects: attachment toward form, appearance, sound, smell, tactile sensations, and so on. All of these individually are powerful enough to cause a lot of problems and difficulties. However, the strongest form of attachment seems to be sexual attachment. Here we find attachment toward all the five senses involved. Therefore, it is all the more powerful and has the potential for problems and destruction.

Because we all share an identical need for love, it is possible to feel that anybody we meet in whatever circumstances, is a brother or sister.

To counter anger, you should cultivate love and compassion.

Love and compassion are states of mind cultivated through efforts to relieve the sufferings of one's fellow human beings.

We need to share with other people because that kind of friendship is something very special.

If in the midst of your enjoyment of the world you have a moment, try to help in however small a way those who are downtrodden and those who, for whatever reason, cannot or do not help themselves. Try not to turn away from those whose appearance is disturbing, from the ragged and unwell. Try never to think of them as inferior to yourself. If you can, try not even to think of yourself as better than the humblest beggar. You will look the same in your grave.

MINDFULNESS

Meditation is the key to spiritual growth.

If you want to change the world, first try to improve and bring about change within yourself. That will help change your family. From there it just gets bigger and bigger. Everything we do has some effect, some impact.

Open your arms to change, but don't let go of your values.

At times there have been impossible responsibilities and a lot of difficulties. Then again, personally I'm quite jovial, with not much worry. I do my best, which is moderation, and failure doesn't matter.

The restlessness and unhappiness that occurs at the level of the mind is something that can only be addressed by a means that is mental.

Change only takes place through action. Frankly speaking, not through prayer or meditation, but through action.

If one's life is simple, contentment has to come. Simplicity is extremely important for happiness. Having few desires, feeling satisfied with what you have, is very vital: satisfaction with just enough food, clothing, and shelter to protect yourself from the elements. And finally, there is an intense delight in abandoning faulty states of mind and in cultivating helpful ones in meditation.

We can live without religion and meditation, but we cannot survive without human affection.

Some stories of Jesus Christ seem miracles. But from the Buddhist viewpoint they are explainable through an inner element. There are five external elements, but there are also five internal elements. Through meditation we can change things and influence one another. So miracles can be explained.

Buddhism has long argued for the tremendous potential for transformation that exists naturally in the human mind. To this end, the tradition has developed a wide range of contemplative techniques, or meditation practices, aimed specifically at two principal objectives: the cultivation of a compassionate heart and the cultivation of deep insights into the nature of reality, which are referred to as the union of compassion and wisdom.

A person who knows a lot but does not practice is like a shepherd who does not own any cattle but always looks after a flock of sheep or cattle. Therefore, studying, reflecting, and meditation on the nature of reality is of great significance for the progress of a spiritual practitioner.

People should remain in society and carry out their usual profession. While contributing to society, they should internally carry on analysis and practice. In daily life, one should go to the office, work, and return home. It would be worthwhile to sacrifice some late evening entertainment, go to sleep early, and get up early the next morning to perform analytical meditation.

In my experience, there is too much emphasis on what is minor and not on what is essential, and what is essential involves being able to transform the individual from within.

If we examine ourselves every day with mindfulness and mental alertness checking our thoughts, motivations, and their manifestations in external behavior, a possibility for change and self-improvement can open within us. Although I myself cannot claim with confidence to have made any remarkable progress over the years, my desire and determination to change and improve is always firm. From early morning until I go to bed and in all situations in life, I always try to check my motivation and be mindful and present in the moment. Personally, I find this to be very helpful in my own life.

Through a difficult period you can learn; you can develop inner strength, determination and courage to face the problems.

We can change; our ultimate nature is pure.

When things are desperate, there is no need to pretend that everything is beautiful. You have to accept reality. This has helped me come closer to reality.

First, one must change. I first watch myself, check myself, then expect change from others.

Problems arise when one falls too deeply into self-regard, when an individual is prepared to exploit or to totally sacrifice other's well-being in the pursuit of self-interest.

Tibetans have a saying: If bad news comes, you listen here (points to the right ear) and let it out here (points to the left ear).

What do we understand by meditation? From the Buddhist point of view, meditation is a spiritual discipline, and one that allows you to have some degree of control over your thoughts and emotions.

For me, it is nothing. New millennium or new century or new year. For me it is another day, another day and night. The sun, the moon, the stars remain the same.

Sooner or later you will find a limitation of resources and will have to adopt a more contented lifestyle.

Old friends pass away, new friends appear. It is just like the days. An old day passes, a new day arrives. The important thing is to make it meaningful: a meaningful friend—or a meaningful day.

Time passes unhindered. When we make mistakes, we cannot turn the clock back and try again. All we can do is use the present well.

We believe the whole world will come and disappear, come and disappear—so eventually the world becomes desert and even the ocean dries up. But then again, another new world is reborn. It's endless.

It looks like there is awful lot of work to do. If you had to analyze all your dreams there would be no time left to dream.

At daybreak if the weather is fine, I go into the garden. This time of day is very special to me. The sky is clear, I see the stars, and I have this special feeling of my insignificance in the cosmos, the realization of what we Buddhists call impermanence.

So long as I am alive, my time and my life must be utilized properly. Then after my death, I don't care how people remember me.

It is crucial to be mindful of death—to contemplate that you will not remain long in this life.

I think when tragic things happen, it is on the surface. It's like the ocean. On the surface a wave comes, and sometimes the wave is very serious and strong. But it comes and goes, comes and goes, and underneath the ocean always remains calm.

So, the tendency of our childish nature is to take small things too seriously and get easily offended, whereas when we are confronted with situations that have long-term consequences, we tend to take things less seriously.

One thing can't be doubted, the "possibility of a quality" is within us. It is called prajana. We can deny everything, except that we have the possibility of being better. Simply reflect on that.

Environmental damage is often gradual and not easily apparent, and by the time we become aware of it, it is generally too late.

COMPASSION

G enuine compassion is unbiased.

My message is the practice of compassion, love, and kindness. Compassion can be put into practice if one recognizes the fact that every human being is a member of humanity and the human family regardless of differences in religion, culture, color, and creed. Deep down there is no difference.

Be kind whenever possible...It is always possible.

Some people, when we talk about compassion and love, think it is a religious matter. Compassion is the universal religion.

If you want others to be happy, practice compassion. If you want to be happy, practice compassion.

In external appearances, there are differences between us and, of course, in religious faith, there are cultural differences between us. But these are all minor. Human compassion does not come from religious text. Human compassion is in our blood.

A good mind, a good heart, warm feel-ings—these are the most important things.

Be a nice person. Be a good person.

The roots of all goodness lie in the soil of appreciation for goodness.

There is no need for temples, no need for complicated philosophies. My brain and my heart are my temples; my philosophy is kindness.

To deepen your gratitude toward all people, it is helpful to reflect on the unintended kindness of those who provide goods and services without necessarily knowing the names or faces of those whom they service. In this life there are so many facilities we enjoy—nice buildings, roads, and so forth—that are produced by other people.

Right from the moment of our birth, we are under the care and kindness of our parents and then later on in our life when we are oppressed by sickness and become old, we are again dependent on the kindness of others. Since at the beginning and end of our lives we are so dependent on others' kindness, how can it be that in the middle we neglect kindness toward others?

Just be a nice warm person, that's enough.

There's no shop that sells kindness; you must build it within. You can transplant hearts, but you cannot transplant a warm heart.

One who smiles has a happy, successful life.

For our life to be of value, I think we must develop basic good human qualities—warmth, kindness, compassion. Then our life becomes meaningful and more peaceful.

I have found that the greatest degree of inner tranquility comes from the development of love and compassion. The more we care for the happiness of others, the greater is our own sense of well-being. Cultivating a close, warm-hearted feeling for others automatically puts the mind at ease. It is the ultimate source of success in life.

Judge your success by what you had to give up in order to get it.

A simple smile. That's the start of opening your heart and being compassionate to others.

The most important thing is to promote compassion and positivism.

It is not enough to be compassionate. You must act. There are two aspects to action. One is to overcome the distortions and afflictions of your own mind, that is, in terms of calming and eventually dispelling anger. This is action out of compassion. The other is more social, more public. When something needs to be done in the world to rectify the wrongs, if one is really concerned with benefiting others, one needs to be engaged, involved.

Tashi Delek. (Tibetan for "Good Wishes")

A truly compassionate attitude toward others does not change even if they behave negatively or hurt you. Whether one believes in a religion or not, and whether one believes in rebirth or not, there isn't anyone who doesn't appreciate kindness and compassion.

Compassion is not religious business, it is human business, it is not luxury, it is essential for our own peace and mental stability, it is essential for human survival.

We don't give our compassion to such and such a person by choice. We give it spontaneously, entirely, without hoping for anything in exchange. And we give it universally.

Genuine compassion involves analyzing the situation regardless of whether the person is close or not.

Merely thinking that compassion and reason and patience are good will not be enough to develop them. We must wait for difficulties to arise and then attempt to practice them.

Mothers in society are the first lamas, or gurus, of compassion; our spiritual lamas come later in life. Our mothers teach us the power and value of compassion right from our birth.

History shows that most of the positive or beneficial developments in human society have occurred as the result of care and compassion. Consider, for example, the abolition of the slave trade...Ideals are the engine of progress.

In the practice of tolerance, one's enemy is the best teacher.

Given human beings' love for truth, justice, peace, and freedom, creating a better, more compassionate world is a genuine possibility. The potential is there.

A mind committed to compassion is like an overflowing reservoir—a constant source of energy, determination, and kindness.

To say violence is bad is not sufficient. We must make an effort to have greater human compassion.

Through these decades, the most important factor for sustaining my peace of mind is compassion.

The essential feature of true compassion is that it is universal and not discriminatory.

We need a little more compassion, and if we cannot have it, then no politician or even a magician can save the planet.

I'm trying to promote the value of compassion and not just based on attachment to those who are close to you but rather for all beings, irrespective of what that person does to you, or whether they are your enemy or not.

Compassion is not helpless pity, but an awareness and determination that demands action.

For people to focus on "my life", "my life", "my life" destroys the capacity for compassion. From that perspective, a small problem appears to be a gigantic problem and only brings more unhappiness, frustration, insecurity, and fear.

Compassion can be roughly defined in terms of a state of mind that is nonviolent and non-harming, or nonaggressive. Because of this there is a danger of confusing compassion with attachment and intimacy.

Compassion, respect, and a sense of understanding know no national boundaries.

[Education and compassion]…if you combine these two, your whole life will be constructive and happy.

The interest in Buddhism is still very strong. So, therefore, the Tibetan Buddhist culture can help to promote…more compassion. And if the most populous nation can become more compassionate—that, I think, would be a very wonderful thing.

International relations seem to lack compassionate virtues. It is all geopolitical considerations and no moral principles.

Great compassion and wisdom are the chief qualities of the Buddha. Even in worldly terms, the more intelligent and knowledgeable a person is, the more the person commands respect. Similarly, the more compassionate, kind, and gentle a person, the more he or she should be respected. So if you are able to develop that intelligence and altruism to their fullest extent, then you are truly admirable and deserve to be respected.

It is easier to generate compassion while visualizing a sentient being who is very destitute, but we need also to reflect on persons who do not seem to be suffering at all, but who are in truth acting in ways that will eventually bring about manifest suffering.

One aspect of compassion is to respect other's rights and to respect other's views. That is the basis for reconciliation. The human spirit of reconciliation based on compassion is working deep down, whether the person really knows it or not. Our basic nature is gentleness; therefore, no matter how much we go through violence and other bad things, ultimately the proper solution is to return to human feeling and affection. So affection or compassion is not only a religious matter, but in our day-to-day life it is quite indispensable.

A heart full of love and compassion is the main source of inner strength, willpower, happiness, and mental tranquility.

Only a spontaneous feeling of empathy with others can really inspire us to act on their behalf. Nevertheless, compassion does not arise mechanically. Such a sincere feeling must grow gradually, cultivated within each individual, based on their own conviction of its worth. Adopting a kind attitude thus becomes a personal matter. How each of us behaves in daily life is, after all, the real test of compassion.

Compassion, a sense of caring, thinking about others' welfare. That sort of attitude brings me inner peace. It has defined the purpose of my life.

True compassion is not just an emotional response but also a firm commitment founded on reason. Therefore, a truly compassionate attitude toward others does not change even if they behave negatively. Through universal altruism, you develop a feeling of responsibility for others: they wish to help them actively overcome their problems.

No matter what the circumstances, no matter what kind of tragedy I am facing, I practice compassion. This gives me inner strength and happiness. This gives me the feeling that my life is useful.

Young people should learn more about the outside world, develop compassion and understanding of others, and practice having patience.

With care and compassion, a warm heart and determination, difficult things can change and healthy, happy people can talk through their differences, reaching a compromise that all can live with.

HAPPINESS

I believe that the purpose of life is to be happy.

From all points of view we're the same in wanting happiness and not wanting suffering. Now oneself is only one, but others are infinite in number. Therefore, others are more important than oneself.

Happiness is not something ready-made. It comes from your own actions.

I don't think a person should have two sides—a private and a public side. There should be no gap; that is not honest.

The fact that there is always a positive side to life is the one thing that gives me a lot of happiness. This world is not perfect. There are problems. But things like happiness and unhappiness are relative. Realizing this gives you hope.

Working to ease the suffering of sentient beings, to improve the situation on the planet, is the only way to happiness, contentment, and peace.

While you are engaging in the practice of giving you should do so with great happiness and radiance on your face. One should practice giving with a smile and with mental uprightness.

If people everywhere are not allowed to strive for the happiness they instinctively want, then they will be dissatisfied and will make problems for everyone. Unless we can create an atmosphere of genuine cooperation—cooperation not gained by threat or force but by heartfelt understanding—life will become ever more difficult. If we can satisfy people at a heart level, peace will ensue. Without the basis of coexistence, if undesirable social, political, and cultural forms continue to be imposed upon people, peace becomes difficult.

When people get angry they lose all sense of happiness. Even if they are good-looking and normally peaceful, their faces turn livid and ugly. Anger upsets their physical well-being and disturbs their rest; it destroys their appetites and makes them age prematurely. Happiness, peace, and sleep evade them, and they no longer appreciate people who have helped them and deserve their trust and gratitude.

I believe that the very purpose of our life is to seek happiness. That is clear. Whether one believes in religion or not, whether one believes in this religion or that religion, we all are seeking something better in life. So, I think, the very motion of our life is toward happiness.

You are welcome whether you're a practicing Buddhist or not. You are seeking happiness and relief from suffering and pain.

If we compare the mental and physical levels of happiness, we find that the experiences of pain and pleasure that take place mentally are actually more powerful.

There are three types of joyous effort: armor like joyous effort: joyous effort in gathering virtues; and joyous effort in working for others.

The interest toward inner values is increasing. People have lots of material goods but are not happy. People are beginning to realize that material facility alone is not the full answer of life. That's my impression.

The road to happiness is rigged with land mines. These are destructive emotions that cause pain and suffering and can be triggered at any time by people whose minds are not trained to apply antidotes to overpower the negative with the positive.

It is essential to know that to be a happy person, happy family, a happy society, it is very crucial to have a good heart.

One can't achieve happiness merely through education and knowledge, though they are important, but should also involve compassion and nonviolence.

Practicing patience is going to bring you long-term benefits. Therefore you should greet the opportunity with great happiness.

I often believe that the basic goal or end of life is happiness, satisfaction. I believe our existence is very much based on hope.

The basic sources of happiness are a good heart, compassion, and love. If we have these mental attitudes, even if we are surrounded by hostility, we feel little disturbance. On the other hand, if we lack compassion and our mental state is filled with anger or hatred, we will not have peace.

A very poor, underprivileged person might think that it would be wonderful to have an automobile or a television set, and should he acquire them, at the beginning he would feel very happy. Now if such happiness were something permanent, it would remain forever. But it does not; it goes. After a few months he wants to change the models. The old ones, the same objects, now cause dissatisfaction. This is the nature of change.

Happiness is a state of mind. With physical comforts…if your mind is still in a state of confusion and agitation, it is not happiness. Happiness means calmness of mind.

One of the characteristics of karmic theory is that there is a definite commensurate relationship between cause and effect. There is no way that negative actions or unwholesome deeds can result in joy and happiness. Joy and happiness, by definition, are the results of fruits of wholesome actions. So from that point of view, it is possible for us to admire not so much the immediate action, but the real cause of joy.

I don't know whether the universe, with its countless galaxies, stars, and planets, has a deeper meaning or not, but at the very least, it is clear that we humans who live on this earth face the task of making a happy life for ourselves. Therefore, it is important to discover what will bring about the greatest degree of happiness.

As human beings we all want to be happy and free from misery…we have learned that the key to happiness is inner peace. The greatest obstacles to inner peace are disturbing emotions such as anger and attachment, fear and suspicion, while love, compassion, and a sense of universal responsibility are the sources of peace and happiness.

Human happiness and human satisfaction must ultimately come from within oneself. It is wrong to expect some final satisfaction to come from money or from a computer.

The purpose of life is happiness whether you are a believer or nonbeliever.

We must not neglect our inner values. If we become slaves of money, we can't be a happy person. If we expect all our problems to be solved by external means, that is a mistake.

We should not be too concerned with our fame or what people say about us, either bad or good because in reality, fame could not make any serious difference to one's life. Therefore, we should have our priorities right, and seek what is truly of value, what is truly of meaning to our life not just mere fame, which is, after all, empty sounds. Some individuals sacrifice many of their material possessions, wealth and even their lives to achieve fame. This type of obsession with seeking fame is very childish and is quite foolish.

Life's purpose of happiness can be gained only if people cultivate the basic human values of compassion, caring, and forgiveness.

Our intention should not be spoiled by the eight worldly preoccupations: gain or loss, pleasure or pain, praise or criticism, and fame or infamy.

It is possible to divide every kind of happiness and suffering into two main categories: mental and physical. Of the two, it is the mind that exerts the greatest influence on most of us.

SPIRITUALITY

We speak of types of faith. The first is faith in the form of admiration that you have toward a particular person or a particular state of being. The second is aspiring faith. There is a sense of emulation—you aspire to attain that state of being. The third type is the faith of conviction.

Faith leads you to a higher state of existence, whereas reason and analysis lead you to full liberation.

I believe deeply that we must find, all of us together, a new spirituality. This new concept universal responsibility ought to be elaborated alongside the religions, in such a way that all people of good will could adhere to it. We ought to promote this concept with the help of scientists. It could lead us to what we are looking for.

Seeking blessings from outsiders is not right. Your life is on your own shoulders. Blind faith is not healthy.

At the end of the last century, science and spirituality seemed incompatible. Now, they have moved closer together.

Faith is the basis of the Path,
The mother of virtues,
Nourishing and growing all good ways,
Cutting away the net of doubt,
Freeing from the torrent of passion…
Faith can assure arrival at enlightenment.

Spirituality should be able to guide people about the essence, which is contentment, self-discipline, caring, sharing, forgiveness, and tolerance.

Once you really make the effort to practice, then you really get the value of religious faith.

Blessings are not enough. Blessings must come from within. Without your own effort, it is impossible for blessings to come.

For proper development I feel that we need a well-balanced education. We need inner spiritual development to acquire a warm heart, which is the basic requirement.

In order to have genuine faith, you need to have one truth, one religion. But that does not mean you lose respect for those of other traditions.

I feel that the essence of spiritual practice is your attitude toward others. When you have a pure, sincere motivation, then you have the right attitude toward others based on kindness, compassion, love, and respect. Practice brings the clear realization of the oneness of all human beings and the importance of others benefiting by your actions.

Many people still consider science and religion to be in opposition. While I agree that certain religious concepts conflict with scientific facts and principles, I also feel that people from both worlds can have an intelligent discussion, one that has the power ultimately to generate a deeper understanding of challenges we face together in our interconnected world.

Faith is the basis of the Path, the mother of virtues, nourishing and growing all good ways, cutting away the net of doubt, freeing from the torrent of passion...Faith can assure arrival at enlightenment.

My plea is that we bring our spirituality, the full richness and simple wholesomeness of our basic human values, to bear upon the course of science and the direction of technology in human society. In essence, science and spirituality, though differing in their approaches, share the same end, which is the betterment of humanity.

Every faith has a piece of the truth.

The essence of all spiritual life is your emotion, your attitude toward others. Once you have pure and sincere motivation, all the rest follows. You can develop this right attitude toward others on the basis of kindness, love, and respect, and on the clear realization of the oneness of all human beings.

Inner darkness, which we call ignorance, is the root of suffering. The more inner light that comes, the more darkness will diminish. This is the only way to achieve salvation or nirvana.

I still need a lot of spiritual improvement in myself.

Faith dispels doubt and hesitation, it liberates you from suffering, and delivers you to the city of peace and happiness. It is faith that removes the mental turbidity and makes your mind clear. Faith reduces your pride and is the root of veneration. It is the supreme lake because you can easily traverse from one stage of the spiritual path to another. It is like your hand, which can gather all virtuous qualities.

I always take the essential part of religion and culture, what is truly useful in our daily lives. This must be distinguished from the ceremonial part and from social habit.

Spirituality is like a medicine. To heal the illness, it is not sufficient to look at the medicine and talk about it. You have to ingest it.

The ultimate authority must always rest with the individual's own reason and critical analysis.

Through blessings, my whole day's thought becomes something useful, also something positive.

RELIGION

If you have a particular faith or religion, that is good. But you can survive without it.

Religions must serve humanity, not the other way around.

All the great religions deserve respect and, if practiced seriously, are paths to love and peace.

The spiritual discovery of people of other faiths is the greatest challenge of the twenty-first century. Some will see this as a threat to identity, others will see this as a completion of identity, the discovery of lost cousins and their worlds. The essence of humility.

Wherever you are, your religious teaching must be there with you.

Most people believe that following the path of compassion and nonviolence is something related to religion. In fact, these are secular ethics and have nothing to do with religion.

Whether Islamic, Hindu, Christian, or Buddhist, religion should not matter.

All religions are essentially the same in their goal of developing a good human heart so that we may become better human beings.

Sometimes religion becomes yet another source for more division and sometimes open conflict. Because of that situation, I feel the different religious traditions have a great responsibility to provide peace of mind and a sense of brotherhood and sisterhood among humanity.

You should respect other religions...the essence of all religions is basically the same: to achieve a true sense of brotherhood, a good heart, respect for others. If we can develop these qualities from within our heart, then I think we can actually achieve true peace.

All religions are meant in principle to help human beings to become better, more refined, and more creative people.

Most people do not derive their values directly from religious traditions. Given that reality, a system of secular moral ethics must be taught to lift the lives and spirits of millions of people.

All major religions have the same potential to create good human beings.

We must make a clear distinction between religious institutions and the practice of religion. Religious institutions and politics should stay apart.

There are philosophical differences, in the concept of a creator, for example. Buddhism is most suitable to me, but not necessarily to everybody. We need pluralism.

If you practice your own religion very intensely, it is easier for you to see the values of other religions.

Every religion has certain unique ideas or techniques and learning about them can only enrich one's own faith.

The world's religions can contribute to world peace, if there is peace and growing harmony between different faiths.

I always believe that it is much better to have a variety of religions, a variety of philosophies, rather than one single religion or philosophy. This is necessary because of the different mental dispositions of each human being. Each religion has certain unique ideas or techniques, and learning about them can only enrich one's own faith.

Those who wage war in the name of religion have failed to look beyond their religion to other faiths they oppose. If they did examine other faiths, they would recognize the same desire for transformation.

Although the world's major religions have different theologies and traditions, they share a common goal of compassion and peace.

I promote harmony on the basis of mutual respect for every religion.

While the concept of one religion or one truth is essential for an individual practitioner, in terms of humanity the concept of several religions is important.

In religion there are no national boundaries. A religion can and should be used by any people or person who finds it beneficial.

All major religion carry the same messages— of love, compassion, forgiveness, tolerance, contentment, and self-discipline. I have Muslim friends, Christian friends. All have these same values.

It does not matter whether you are a theist or atheist, what matters is sincerity, forgiveness, and compassion.

The very purpose of religion is to control yourself, not to criticize others. Rather, we must criticize ourselves. How much am I doing about my anger? About my attachment, about my hatred, about my pride, my jealousy? These are the things which we must check in daily life.

If you follow any (religious) practice, your mind becomes more compassionate and calm, more peaceful, and your mental function becomes more effective.

I speak to you as just another human being; as a simple monk. If you find what I say useful, then I hope you will try to practice it.

All of the different religious faiths, despite their philosophical differences, have a similar objective. Every religion emphasizes human improvement, love, respect for others, sharing other people's suffering. On these lines every religion has more or less the same viewpoint and the same goal.

People who call themselves religious without basic human values like compassion; they are not really religious people.

I think all religions have the same potential to strengthen human values and to develop general harmony.

BUDDHISM

Tibetan Buddhism is at one level the universal message similarly offered by Christianity—love thy neighbor as thyself.

Buddhism does not recognize a creator of the universe—no single God—but rather it subscribes to a boundless continuum that had no beginning and will have no end.

Buddhism relies more on one's own effort, on reason rather than faith.

The practice of morality—which means guarding your three doors of body, speech, and mind from indulging in unwholesome activities—equips you with mindfulness and conscientiousness. Therefore, morality is the foundation of the Buddhist path.

The true test of honoring Buddhas or God is the love one extends to fellow humans.

Karma means action. So things change through action not by prayer…not by wish.

Basically, the Buddhist attitude is that you should not accept certain things through sheer faith. And for that you need a skeptical attitude. Buddha himself made this clear to his followers. He said you should not accept those things I taught out of respect for me, but rather through investigation by yourself.

In Buddhism we have relative truth and absolute truth.

Your enlightenment rests on your own shoulders.

Whatever we say, let us speak clearly and to the point, in a voice that is calm and pleasant, unaffected by attachment or hatred. Look kindly at others, thinking: it is thanks to them that I shall attain Buddhahood.

If advertising is for a good cause, it is worthwhile. Buddha advertised enlightenment or nirvana. If it is reasonable and beneficial, it is good, but if it is only for profit, cheating, and exploitation, or is misleading, then it is wrong.

The seed for nirvana exists in all of us. The time has come to think more wisely, hasn't it?

Through meditative techniques, one can free the mind of delusions and attain what we call enlightenment.

But...then as a Buddhist, as my own motivation is concerned, I [try to be] open and sincere and try my best. If something is achieved, very good, if not achieved, no regrets.

I just want to live as a simple Buddhist monk, but during the last thirty years I have made many friends around the world and I want to have close contact with these people. I want to contribute to harmony and peace of mind, for less conflict. Wherever the possibility is, I'm ready. This is my life's goal.

I always consider myself first and foremost to be a monk. A Buddhist monk. Dalai Lama comes after that.

The Buddhist uses the Buddha's words only as a key. We emphasize human reason...and our own experience in determining if we find something convincing and reliable.

A Tibetan wanderer would regard a jumbo jet—or television—to be a miracle. But to a scientist who knows how they work, they're not. Similarly, there are certain things that can be done through mental training. To those who have developed skills it's nothing special.

From a believer's point of view I do have some special relationship with some higher beings. But in my own mind I am still an ordinary Buddhist monk.

Often I have some kind of desire to go to a very remote area. When I listen to a Tibetan who has stayed in these mountains and they tell me about their way of life, in a bare room, just empty with no gold or bronze, I very much envy it.

The main idea of Buddhism is the unification of the body, mind, and spirit, and it is only by attaining such a state that people can find happiness in life.

In my mind I am a monk, a Buddhist monk. You see one indication is in my dream, sometimes certain dreams happen, then immediately is the feeling, always, I am monk. In dreamtime I never felt I am Dalai Lama.

Buddhist culture provides for a gentler attitude toward nature and toward other human beings.

According to Buddhist belief, every sentient being has a mind whose fundamental nature is essentially pure and unpolluted by mental distortions. We refer to that nature as the seed of enlightenment.

Achieving nirvana brings freedom from the endless cycle of suffering caused by wanting too much money, of seeking too much power, of trying to find happiness through sensual pleasures.

The essence of Buddhism is if you can, help others. If not, then at least refrain from hurting others.

While for certain religions the principal practice is to recite prayers and for others it is mainly physical penance, in Buddhism the crucial practice is understood to be transforming and improving the mind.

If science proves some belief of Buddhism wrong, then Buddhism will have to change. In my view, science and Buddhism share a search for the truth and for understanding reality. By learning from science about aspects of reality where its understanding may be more advanced, I believe that Buddhism enriches its own world view.

I believe that spirituality and science are different but complementary investigative approaches with the same greater goal, of seeking the truth. In this, there is much each may learn from the other, and together they may contribute to expanding the horizon of human knowledge and wisdom.

If you are able to transform adverse situations into factors of the spiritual path, hindrances will become favorable conditions for spiritual practice.

Every day, think as you wake up, "Today I am fortunate to have woken up, I am alive, I have a precious human life, I am not going to waste it. I am going to use all my energies to develop myself, to expand my heart out to others, to achieve enlightenment for the benefit of all beings, I am going to have kind thoughts towards others, I am not going to get angry or think badly about others, I am going to benefit others as much as I can."

It may seem unrealistic to think we can ever become free from hatred, but Buddhists have systematic methods for gradually developing a tolerance powerful enough to give such freedom.

As a Buddhist monk, I try to develop compassion myself, not just from a religious point of view, but from a humanitarian one as well. To encourage myself in this altruistic attitude, I sometimes find it helpful to imagine myself, a single individual, on one side and on the other a huge gathering of all other human beings. Then I ask myself, "Whose interests are more important?" To me it is then quite clear that, however important I may feel, I am only one, while others form the majority.

As a Buddhist monk, my concern extends to all members of the human family and, indeed, to all sentient beings who suffer. I believe all suffering is caused by ignorance. People inflict pain on others in the selfish pursuit of their happiness or satisfaction. Yet true happiness comes from a sense of brotherhood and sisterhood.

From the point of view of a practitioner on the path, many of the high levels of realization that you gain and the progress you make on your spiritual journey are dependent upon cooperation and interaction with other sentient beings.

One of Buddhism's most relevant lessons is the avoidance of extremes. It teaches that freedom and happiness will not be found in the extremes of either sensual indulgence or mortification: a middle way must be found.

Buddhism explains that our normal state of mind is such that our thoughts and emotions are wild and unruly, and since we lack the mental discipline needed to tame them, we are powerless to control them. As a result, they control us.

Buddhism is essentially a practical doctrine. In addressing the fundamental problem of human suffering, it does not insist on a single solution.

As a Buddhist, blessing must come from within, not from outside.

In trying to determine the source of one's problems, it seems that the Western approach differs in some respects from the Buddhist approach. Underlying all Western modes of analysis is a very strong rationalistic tendency—an assumption that everything can be accounted for. And on top of that, there are constraints created by certain premises that are taken for granted.

True enlightenment is nothing but the nature of one's own self being fully realized.

If practices from my own tradition (Buddhism) can be brought together with scientific methods, then we may be able to take another small step toward alleviating human suffering.

Buddhahood is a state free of all obstructions to knowledge and disturbing emotions. It is the state in which the mind is fully evolved.

What are reborn are our habits. Enlightenment is the ending of rebirth, which means a complete non-attachment or misidentification with all thoughts, feelings, perceptions, physical sensations, and ideas.

As long as you are not completely enlight-
ened, there will always be an inner obstruc-
tion to knowledge that will make your task of
helping others incomplete.

I myself feel, and also tell other Buddhists,
that the question of nirvana will come later.
There is not much hurry. If in day-to-day
life you lead a good life, honestly, with love,
with compassion, with less selfishness, then
automatically it will lead to nirvana.

According to Buddhism, individuals are
masters of their own destiny. So our future
is in our hands. What greater free will do we
need?

When we talk about gaining the perfect wisdom of a Buddha, we should not think that we need to create qualities in ourselves that are not there already, and acquire them from somewhere outside of us. Rather, we should see perfect Buddha wisdom as a potential that is being realized.

From one point of view we can say that we have human bodies and are practicing the Buddha's teachings and are thus much better than insects. But we can also say that insects are innocent and free from guilt, whereas we often lie and misrepresent ourselves in devious ways in order to achieve our ends or better ourselves. From this perspective, we are much worse than insects.

Tibetan Buddhist goals are the same as those of Western science: to serve humanity and to make better human beings.

In my daily practice as a Buddhist monk I have to observe many rules, but the fundamental theme of them all is a deep concern and respect for the rights of others.

It is only after mature reflection (that) you (should) believe that Buddhism could offer you more than Christianity (and then) that you should become a Buddhist.

Laziness will stop your progress in your spiritual practice. One can be deceived by three types of laziness: the laziness of indolence, which is the wish to procrastinate; laziness of inferiority, which is doubting your capabilities; and the laziness that is attached to negative actions, or putting great effort into non-virtue.

In some respects I have been the most unlucky Dalai Lama because I have spent more time living as a refugee outside of my country than I have spent in Tibet. On the other hand, it has been very rewarding for me to live in a democracy and to learn about the world in a way we Tibetans had never known before.

In the Buddhist tradition, you would aspire to Buddhahood. In the Christian context you may not use the same language, but you can say you aspire to attain the perfection of the divine nature, or union with God. I believe that our Tibetan ability to combine spiritual qualities with a realistic and practical attitude enables us to make a special contribution, in however modest in a way.

In Buddhism we have a concept called interdependency. It is very relevant today. Simply put it says that my future is linked to that of society, that of human beings to the environment.

HUMANITY

I believe that to meet the challenges of our times, human beings will have to develop a greater sense of universal responsibility. Each of us must learn to work not just for oneself, one's own family or one's nation, but for the benefit of all humankind. Universal responsibility is the key to human survival. It is the best foundation for world peace.

To me there is no difference, whether president, beggar, or king.

We are the same human beings; we have the same experience. As far as human rights are concerned, there are no differences between rich and poor, or educated and uneducated, even the Queen of England and the beggar in the street.

Every human being should realize that the future of humanity is dependent on their present actions and thinking.

I think now the time has come to think more of humanity than of my nation or that nation. Then automatically, through such a manner of thinking, each individual mind is open.

If you have a sincere and open heart, you naturally feel self-worth and confidence, and there is no need to be fearful of others. If you have this basic quality of kindness or good heart, then all other things, education, ability will go in the right direction.

Humans are not machines—we are something more. We have feeling and experience. Material comforts are not sufficient to satisfy us. We need something deeper—human affection.

There is too little contact among world leaders.

I believe that to meet the challenges of our times, human beings will have to develop a greater sense of universal responsibility. Each of us must learn to work not just for oneself, one's own family or one's nation, but for the benefit of all humankind. Universal responsibility is the key to human survival. It is the best foundation for world peace.

Human rights should be universal.

Our beautiful blue planet has no national boundaries.

Every human being should realize that the future of humanity is dependent on their present actions and thinking.

We are the same human beings; we have the same experience. As far as human rights are concerned, there are no differences between rich and poor, or educated and uneducated, even the Queen of England and the beggar in the street.

The future depends on the present.

It is my fundamental belief that all human beings share the same basic aspirations: that we all want happiness and that we all share suffering. Asians, just like Americans, Europeans, and the rest of the world share a desire to live life to its fullest, to better ourselves and the lives of our loved ones.

I pray for a more friendly, more caring, and more understanding human family on this planet. To all who dislike suffering, who cherish lasting happiness, this is my heartfelt appeal.

The desire for democracy and freedom is an innate human desire. No force can stop that.

When I say that human nature is gentleness, it is not 100 percent so. Every human being has that nature, but there are many people acting against their nature, being false.

Our planet is blessed with vast natural treasures. If we use them wisely, beginning with the elimination of militarism and war, every human being will be able to live a healthy, prosperous existence.

Freedom is a human need; it may be even more than human. I have a cat. People feed this cat; they pet this cat; they give the cat everything he needs. But every time the window is open just a little, he runs away.

127

Ultimately there are no dualities—neither black nor white, neither oppressor nor victim. We are all connected in a journey toward the happiness that is labeled enlightenment.

In any human society where you want and need progress, it is essential to have freedom.

Among the many forces in which the human spirit has tried to express its innermost yearnings and perceptions, music is perhaps the most universal. It symbolizes humanity's search for harmony, with oneself and others, with nature, and with the spiritual and sacred within and around us.

In the interests of everyone, of humanity, the artist has a responsibility to use his medium well. In the Tibetan culture, most of the paintings are of deities or Buddhas and they try to send a message of value of the spiritual.

We have to treat the whole world as one entity. There is no possibility of remaining isolated from the rest of humanity.

Our strength is truth, justice, reason, and human understanding.

Respect for fundamental human rights should not remain an ideal to be achieved but a requisite foundation for every human society.

All human beings come from a mother's womb. We are all the same part of one human family. We should have a clear realization of the oneness of all humanity.

Only a small proportion of the world's 5 billion people are engaged in acts of violence. The overwhelming majority are engaged in acts of loving, caring, and sharing.

I believe that any human activity which stems from basic gentleness and the nonviolent nature of human beings...has the guarantee to be of benefit and service. And any act... even if the aim or goal be a noble one, so long as the act is motivated by a feeling of hatred, a feeling of revenge, then I don't think it will have benefit.

As long as we are on this small planet together, we need human gentleness, human affection.

Despite all differences of class or ideology, mentally, emotionally, we all have the same basic nature.

131

Compared to the major illnesses in the world, my headache is much better.

I try to see each tragedy in the context of other bigger tragedies in history. That gives me a larger focus and makes it easier to bear. So that is my secret, my trick.

Our problems, though grave and complex, are within our own power to control and rectify. The solution can only be based upon an approach that transcends selfish and regional demands.

Humanity in this century has seen many wonders, such as technological developments, but it has also seen the greatest number of humanity killed through violence and war.

I believe that in the twentieth century, humanity has learned from many, many experiences. Some positive and many negative. What misery, what destruction! The greatest number of human beings were killed in the two world wars. But human nature is such that when we face a tremendous situation, the human mind can wake up and find some other alternative. That is a human capacity.

War, the desire to destroy one's enemy, is an outmoded concept, especially now, when the interest of all the world's people is so linked. If you hit another being, it is like hitting part of your own body.

Everyone spent a few months in their mother's womb, but nobody remembers that. So one does not necessarily remember everything about one's existence.

When you think about hope and humanity the mind opens.

Without a sense of universal responsibility, our very existence and survival becomes threatened.

Whether they belong to more evolved species like humans, or to simpler ones such as animals, all beings primarily seek peace, comfort, and security. Life is as dear to the mute animal as it is to any human being. Even the simplest insect strives for protection from dangers that threaten its life. Just as each one of us wants to live and does not wish to die, so it is with all other creatures in the universe.

Just as the world of business has been paying renewed attention to ethics, the world of science would benefit from more deeply considering the implications of its own work. Scientists should be more than merely technically adept; they should be mindful of their own motivation and the larger goal of what they do: the betterment of humanity.

I hope that you at this moment will think of yourself as a human being rather than as an American, Asian, European, African, or member of any particular country. These loyalties are secondary. If you and I find common ground as human beings, we will communicate on a basic level.

The whole world has now become like one family, almost like one body. So some destruction of some other part of the world is actually destruction of yourself.

We all desire freedom, but what distinguishes human beings is their intelligence. As free human beings we can use our unique intelligence to try to understand our world and ourselves.

We can see that all the desirable experiences that we cherish or aspire to attain are dependent upon cooperation and interaction with other sentient beings.

137

If the basic human nature was aggressive, we would be born with animal claws and huge teeth—but ours are very short, very pretty, very weak. That means we are not well equipped to be aggressive beings. Even the size of our mouth is very small. So I think the basic nature of human beings should be gentle.

The fundamental cause of suffering is ignorance—the mistaken apprehension that living beings and objects inherently exist.

The practice of altruism is the authentic way of conducting human life, and is not limited to the religious.

We must find a way to present basic human values to everyone—and present them not as religious matters but as secular ethics that are essential whether you are religious or not.

In this century we have made remarkable material progress, but basically we are the same as we were thousands of years ago. Our spiritual needs are still very great.

Basically we are all the same human beings with the same potential to be a good human being or a bad human being... The important thing is to realize the positive side and try to increase that; realize the negative side and try to reduce. That's the way.

Good human qualities—honesty, sincerity, a good heart—cannot be bought with money, nor can they be produced by machines, but only by the mind itself. We can call this the inner light, or God's blessing, or human quality. This is the essence of mankind.

From the very core of our being we desire contentment. For harmony each individual's identity must be fully respected.

In every part of the world, there are people who really speak about human rights, and speak about the rights of self-determination, and rights of animals. All of these are, I think, signs of positive change.

The idea that people can live together freely
as individuals, equal in principle and therefore responsible for each other, essentially
agrees with the Buddhist disposition.

Today, more than ever before, life must be
characterized by a sense of universal responsibility, not only to nation to nation and
human to human, but also human to other
forms of life.

Naturally, every action that is destructive is
against human nature. Constructiveness is
the human way. Therefore, I think that in
terms of basic human feeling, violence is not
good. Nonviolence is the only way.

Perhaps you may know that my usual way of meeting with people is completely informal. I think the very purpose of meeting is connection, or contact, person to person. So formality sometimes becomes an additional barrier.

Among the 7 billion human beings, the older generation, including me, is getting ready to say good-bye to this world. The youth has to carry the responsibility for the future. So, please realize your responsibility, remember your potential, and have self-confidence. Have an open mind and a sense of caring and belonging. The freshness and strength that youth has should not fade away. You must keep this enthusiasm.

One of the most powerful visions I have experienced was the first photograph of the Earth from outer space. The image of a blue planet floating in deep space, glowing like the full moon on a clear night, brought home powerfully to me the recognition that we are indeed all members of a single family sharing one little house.

Nowadays the world is becoming increasingly materialistic, and mankind is reaching toward the very zenith of external progress, driven by an insatiable desire for power and vast possessions. Yet by this vain striving for perfection in a world where everything is relative, they wander even further away from inward peace and happiness of the mind.

MAKING A
DIFFERENCE

Each individual has an opportunity to make a difference.

Simply, I try my best to contribute as much as I can my share of responsibility as a human being—that is all.

Be a good human being, a warmhearted, affectionate person. That is my fundamental belief.

I believe in humanity, and its level in a person is more important than his or her belief or faith.

You can develop the right attitude toward others if you have kindness, love, and respect for them, and a clear realization of the oneness of all human beings.

Freedom is the real source of human happiness and creativity. Irrespective of whether you are a believer or nonbeliever, whether Buddhist, Christian, or Jew, the important thing is to be a good human being.

As long as space endures, and for as long as living beings remain, until then may I, too, abide to dispel the misery of the world.

May I become at all times, both now and
   forever
A protector for those without protection
A guide to those who have lost their way
A ship for those with oceans to cross
A bridge for those with rivers to cross
A sanctuary for those in danger
A lamp for those without light
A place of refuge for those who lack shelter
And a servant to all in need.
I'm always against violence.

To be a good human being, that is the most important thing. I myself am also trying to be a good person. Sometimes I fail, but I try. That is a source of one's own happiness.

Through money or power you cannot solve all problems. The problem in the human heart must be solved first.

I believe that because of our intelligence we human beings are also capable of developing infinite altruism.

As long as we are alive as human beings, there is something we can do about it. It is a great mistake to regard this life as fruitless. We have such a wonderful opportunity. We need a little more patience and determination. There is no point in engaging in foolish anxiety.

The mere living is not so important. The important thing is usefulness. So if I could get another hundred years more and be useful, then…good. Otherwise, you just create more problems for others.

Irrespective of past history, I'm always looking forward.

The more we focus on others, the more we have a concern for others, it seems to bring an inner strength.

Many of our troubles are man-made, created by our own ignorance and greed and irresponsible actions.

If you help and serve others, you will ultimately gain.

The main cause of suffering is egoistic desire for one's own comfort and happiness.

It is under the greatest adversity that there exists the greatest potential for doing good, both for oneself and others.

Caring about others is a great benefit for the self.

When I think about the values of altruism, I am often very moved.

If we wish to secure peace for ourselves, we must start by championing it for others.

There is a phenomenological difference in experiencing pain yourself and sharing someone else's pain and suffering. Your own pain is involuntary; you feel overwhelmed and have no control. When feeling the pain of others, there is an element of discomfort, but there also is a level of stability because you are voluntarily accepting pain. It gives you a sense of confidence.

With the realization of ones' own potential and self-confidence in ones' ability, one can build a better world. According to my own experience, self-confidence is very important. That sort of confidence is not a blind one; it is an awareness of ones' own potential. On that basis, human beings can transform themselves by increasing the good qualities and reducing the negative qualities.

Who is more important, you or others? The conclusion is clear; even if minor suffering happens to all others, its range is infinite, whereas when something happens to me, it is limited to just one person. When we look at others in this way, oneself is not so important.

Sensitivity to people's problems, truthfulness, honesty, and a sense of responsibility are vital both for governance and also as a source of satisfaction.

If we carry basic human spirit—human good qualities—then many problems we can reduce, eliminate.

The moment you think only of yourself, the focus of your whole mind narrows, and because of this narrow focus, uncomfortable things can appear huge and bring you fear, discomfort, and a sense of feeling overwhelmed by misery. The moment you think of others with a sense of caring, however, your mind widens. Within that wider angle, your own problems appear to be of no significance, and this makes a big difference.

Helping others is not limited to providing food, shelter, and so forth, but includes relieving the basic causes of suffering and providing the basic causes of happiness.

We must recognize that all beings want the same thing that we want. This is the way to achieve a true understanding, unfettered by artificial consideration.

When you engage in fulfilling the needs of others, your own needs are fulfilled as a by-product.

The self-cherishing attitude makes us very uptight; we think we are extremely important, and our basic desire is for ourselves to be happy and for things to go well for us. Yet we don't know how to bring this about. In fact, acting out of self-cherishing can never make us happy.

In general, I always state that I have three commitments in life. Firstly, on the level of a human being, my first commitment is the promotion of human values such as compassion, forgiveness, tolerance, contentment, and self-discipline.

As long as we live in this world, we are bound to encounter problems. If, at such times, we lose hope and become discouraged, we diminish our ability to face difficulties. If, on the other hand, we remember that it is not just ourselves but also everyone who has to undergo suffering, this more realistic perspective will increase our determination and capacity to overcome troubles.

When in the company of others I shall always consider myself as the lowest of all, and from the depth of my heart hold them dear and supreme.

Human potential is the same for all. Your feeling, "I am not of value," is wrong. Absolutely wrong. You are deceiving yourself. We all have the power of thought—so what are you lacking? If you have willpower, then you can do anything. It is usually said that you are your own master.

I'm just a human being and, incidentally, a Tibetan who chooses to be a Buddhist monk.

It is ironic that the more serious problems emanate from the more industrially advanced societies. Science and technology have worked wonders in many fields, but the basic human problems remain.

In this ever-changing world there are two important things that we should keep in mind. The first is self-examination. We should reexamine our own attitude toward others and constantly check ourselves to see whether we are practicing properly. Before pointing our fingers at others we should point it toward ourselves. Second, we must be prepared to admit our faults and stand corrected.

To renounce the world means to give up your attachment to the world. It does not mean that you have to separate yourself from it. The very purpose of our doctrine is to serve others. In order to serve others you must remain in the society. You should not isolate yourself from the rest.

In one sense, we can say that other sentient beings are really the principal source of all our experiences of joy, happiness, and prosperity.

We need to see each other's suffering as our own.

Try to develop a deep conviction that the present human body has great potential and that you shall never waste even a single minute of its use. Not taking any essence of this precious human existence, but just wasting it, is almost like taking poison while being fully aware of the consequences of doing so. It is very wrong for people to feel deeply sad when they lose money, yet when they waste the precious moments of their lives they do not have the slightest feeling of repentance.

The task of man is to help others; that's my firm teaching, that's my message. That is my own belief. For me, the fundamental question is better relations; better relations among human beings—and whatever I can contribute to that.

By thinking of all sentient beings as even better than the wish-granting gem for accomplishing the highest aim, may I always consider them precious.

First we must help; then, later we can talk about the causes of any tragedy. There is an Indian saying: if you are struck by a poisonous arrow, it is important first to pull it out. There is no time to ask who shot it, what sort of poison it is, and so on. First handle the immediate problem, and later investigate. Similarly, when we encounter human suffering, it is important to respond with compassion rather than to question the politics of those we help.

If you help others with sincere motivation and sincere concern, that will bring you more fortune, more friends, more smiles, and more success. If you forget about others' rights and neglect others welfare, ultimately you will be very lonely.

Our prime purpose in this life is to help others. And if you can't help them, at least don't hurt them.

Because of the interdependent nature of everything, we cannot hope to solve the multifarious problems with a one-sided or self-centered attitude.

Above all, we must put others before us and keep others in our mind constantly: the self must be placed last. All our doings and thinkings must be motivated by compassion for others. The way to acquire this kind of outlook is that we must accept the simple fact that whatever we desire is also desired by others. Every being wants happiness, not suffering. If we adopt a self-centered approach to life by which we attempt to use others for our own self-interest, we might be able to gain temporary benefit, but in the long run, we will not succeed in achieving even our personal happiness, and hope for the next life is out of question.

It seems to me that Western science and Eastern philosophy can join together to create a really complete and full-fledged human being. It is only in this way that man will emerge strengthened from his condition and become whole. What in fact interests me is what is beyond matter and awareness, what really is important and what makes us what we are.

Ideals are very important in one's life. Without ideals you cannot move—whether you achieve them or not is immaterial. But one must try and approximate them.

Think of all sentient beings as being more precious than jewels, examine one's life to avoid negative emotions and harmful actions, and treat enemies as sacred friends.

I always consider all human beings to be special, whether they are educated or uneducated. They all have the same human mind and human spirit and that is what is important.

If objects and people evoke attachment in us, we do not understand the nature of phenomena. We can only become detached by realizing the true nature of things.

COMMUNITY

Because we all share this small planet Earth, we have to live in harmony and peace with each other and with nature. That is not just a dream, but a necessity.

It is always a possibility in a multicultural society to keep an identity. Complete isolation is impractical. You have to mix with the rest of the community in a more balanced way, mixing with the new situations and the modern way while keeping your traditional identity.

Regardless of race, creed, ideology, political bloc (East and West), or economic region (North and South), the most important and basic aspect of all people is their shared humanity—the fact that each person, old, young, rich, poor, educated, uneducated, male or female, is a human. This shared humanness and thus the shared aspiration of gaining happiness and avoiding suffering as well as the basic right to bring these about are of prime importance.

I am optimistic that the ancient values that have sustained mankind are today reaffirming themselves to prepare us for a kinder, happier twenty-first century.

When we develop a close contact among ourselves, it is possible to gain more awareness of each other's tradition. On such a basis, it becomes possible for us to make a combined effort.

I believe that politics becomes dirty because politicians become dirty, even though politics themselves are an instrument to help solve problems in society.

If you shift your focus from oneself to others, and think more about others' well-being and welfare, it has an immediate liberating effect.

Tyranny is essentially against human nature. It can't work. It is against nature's law, so therefore no force can stop human nature winning.

If we each selfishly pursue only what we believe to be in our own interest, without caring about the needs of others, we not only end up harming others but also ourselves.

Political leaders needed to inculcate more spiritual values than those sages living on the mountain tops.

We need to help each other when we have difficulties, and we must share the good fortune that we enjoy.

As more and more people become educated as to their individual potential, the more they seek to express themselves through a democratic system.

My favorite aspect of American culture is the sense of ease with which you interact with people.

Democracy, free elections, a free press, and an independent judiciary, this is the best guarantee for human rights.

In the case of animals, usually from the facial expression one can tell what they are going through, whereas human beings are much more sophisticated. To some extent you can feel it, but often they can be deceptive. For instance, initially they are nice but then they turn out to be bad; whereas in the other case, initially they are horrible but then they turn out to be good and reliable.

The universe that we inhabit and our shared perception of it are the results of a common karma. Likewise, the places that we will experience in future rebirths will be the outcome of the karma that we share with the other beings living there. The actions of each of us, human or nonhuman, have contributed to the world in which we live. We all have a common responsibility for our world and are connected with everything in it.

In the present circumstances, no one can afford to assume that someone else will solve their problems. Every individual has a responsibility to help guide our global family in the right direction. Good wishes are not sufficient; we must become actively engaged.

The earth is, to a certain extent, our mother. She is so kind, because whatever we do, she tolerates it. But now, the time has come when our power to destroy is so extreme that Mother Earth is compelled to tell us to be careful. The population explosion and many other indications make that clear, don't they? Nature has its own natural limitations.

We are all on this planet together. We are all brothers and sisters with the same physical and mental faculties, the same problems, and the same needs. We must all contribute to the fulfillment of the human potential and the improvement of the quality of life as much as we are able. Mankind is crying out for help. Ours is a desperate time. Those who have something to offer should come forward. Now is the time.

PEACE

Without inner peace, it is impossible to have world peace. Through compassion, through love, it is possible to become a true human family. Through love we can have true happiness, real disarmament.

Every person has the same potential for inner tranquility, but negative forces such as fear, suspicion, selfishness, and self-hatred can destroy inner peace.

We can never obtain peace in our outer world until we make peace with ourselves.

Where ignorance is our master, there is no possibility of real peace.

Genuine lasting world peace must come out of mutual trust.

Sacrificing the "nightclub experience" for early morning meditation would make the world a more peaceful place.

You cannot buy peace of mind in a shop—at least not as long as our brains haven't been replaced by computers.

In the East, we need more material goods and development. In the West, you need to develop the mind to sustain happiness and peace, so I think we can benefit from an exchange.

There can be no peace as long as there is grinding poverty, social injustice, inequality, oppression, environmental degradation, and as long as the weak and small continue to be trodden by the mighty and powerful.

Do not confuse peace of mind with spaced-out insensitivity. A truly peaceful mind is very sensitive, very aware.

It is my belief that whereas the twentieth century has been a century of war and untold suffering, the twenty-first century should be one of peace and dialogue.

Human beings are of such nature that they should have not only material facilities but spiritual sustenance as well. Without spiritual sustenance, it is difficult to get and maintain peace of mind.

If we accept that others have a right to peace and happiness equal to our own, do we not have a responsibility to help those in need?

As long as there is no freedom in many parts of the world, there can be no real peace.

Peace starts within each one of us. When we have inner peace, we can be at peace with those around us.

Genuine peace between nations will come from mutual respect, not from weapons or force.

187

Inner peace is the key. If you have inner peace, the external problems do not affect your deep sense of peace and tranquility.

Nearly all of us receive our first lessons in peaceful living from our mothers, because the need for love lies at the very foundation of human existence. From the earliest stages of our growth, we are completely dependent on our mother's care and it is very important for us that she expresses her love. If children do not receive proper affection, in later life they will often find it hard to love others.

There is no doubt about the increase in our material progress and technology, but somehow this is not sufficient, as we have not yet succeeded in bringing about peace and happiness or in overcoming suffering.

It is not possible to find peace in the soul without security and harmony between the people.

WISDOM

I am open to the guidance of synchronicity, and do not let expectations hinder my path.

Share your knowledge. It's a way to achieve immortality.

Remember that silence is sometimes the best answer.

It's best not to get too excited or too depressed by the ups and downs of life.

Spend some time alone every day.

Live a good, honorable life. Then when you get older and think back, you'll be able to enjoy it a second time.

Sometimes more silence is useful.

As far as your personal requirements are concerned, the ideal is to have fewer involvements, fewer obligations and fewer affairs, business or whatever. However, so far as the interest of the larger community is concerned, you must have as many involvements as possible and as many activities as possible.

Through training there is knowledge. You can produce compassion, love, forgiveness. You can change yourself.

Anything that contradicts experience and logic should be abandoned.

The period of greatest gain in knowledge and experience is the most difficult in one's life. Through a difficult period you can learn; you can develop inner strength, determination, and courage to face the problems.

The person who has a tremendous reserve of patience and tolerance has a certain degree of tranquility and calmness in his or her life. Such a person is not only happy and more emotionally grounded, but also seems to be physically healthier and to experience less illness. The person possesses a strong will, has good appetite, and can sleep with a clear conscience.

Sometimes one creates a dynamic impression by saying something, and sometimes one creates as significant an impression by remaining silent.

A learned person will become noble only when he or she has put into real practice what has been learnt, instead of just mere words.

Remember that not getting what you want is sometimes a wonderful stroke of luck.

Occasionally people who do not have a proper knowledge of karmic law say that such and such person is very kind and religious, but he always has problems, whereas so and so is very deceptive and negative, but always seems very successful. Such people may think that there is no karmic law at all. There are others who go to the other extreme and become superstitious, thinking that when someone experiences illness, it is all due to harmful spirits. However, there is a definite relation between causes and effects: that actions not committed will never produce an effect; and that once committed, actions will never lose their potentiality.

Knowledge is important, but much more important is the use toward which it is put. This depends on the heart and mind of the one who uses it.

Smile if you want a smile from another face.

In the face of any real ethical challenge, we must respond in a spirit of humility, recognizing not only the limits of our knowledge (both collective and personal) but also our vulnerability to being misguided in context of such a rapidly changing reality.

I believe that we must find a way to bring ethical considerations to bear upon the direction of scientific development, especially in the life sciences. By invoking fundamental ethical principles, I am not advocating a fusion of religious ethics and scientific inquiry. Rather, I am speaking of what I call "secular ethics," which embrace the principles we share as human beings: compassion, tolerance, consideration of others, the responsible use of knowledge and power. These principles transcend the barriers between religious believers and non-believers; they belong not to one faith, but to all faiths.

When we die, nothing can be taken with us but the seeds of our life's work and our spiritual knowledge.

In our world, we need a clear awareness of the interdependent nature of nations, of humans and animals, and of humans, animals, and the world. Everything is of interdependent nature. I feel that many problems, especially man-made problems, are due to a lack of knowledge about this interdependent nature.

To develop genuine devotion, you must know the meaning of teachings. The main emphasis in Buddhism is to transform the mind, and this transformation depends upon meditation. In order to meditate correctly, you must have knowledge.

If you must be selfish, then be wise and not narrow-minded in your selfishness.

Intelligence has the potential for both happiness and suffering.

You see, the past is past and the future is yet to come. That means the future is in your hands—the future entirely depends on the present. That realization gives you a great responsibility.

I think the ultimate power depends very much on truth. Truthfulness is very essential.

If you have too much expectation, you may come away disappointed.

What science finds to be nonexistent, we must accept as nonexistent; but what science merely does not find is a completely different matter....It is quite clear that there are many, many mysterious things.

Home is where you live, where you can utilize your usefulness.

Tibetans have a saying: Even though a bird can fly, it must land on earth.

203

A young man caught a small bird, and held it behind his back. He then asked, "Master, is this bird I hold in my hands alive or dead?" The boy thought this was a grand opportunity to play a trick on the old man. If the master answered, "dead," it would be let loose into the air. If the master answered "alive," his would simply wring its neck. The master spoke, "The answer is in your hands."

DISAGREEMENTS

Your enemy is your best friend.

People who fight with other human beings out of anger, hatred, and strong emotion, even if they gain victory over their enemies in battle, are not in reality true heroes. What they are doing is slaying corpses, because human beings, being transient, will die. Whether or not these enemies die in the battle is another question, but they will die at some point. So, in reality they are slaying those already destined to die. The true hero is the one who gains victory over hatred and anger.

Within oneself, within each single person, one finds many inconsistencies and contradictions. Sometimes the disparity between one's thoughts early and late in the day is so great that one spends all one's energy trying to figure out how it can be resolved. This can lead to headaches. So naturally, between two persons, between parents and children, between brothers and sisters, there are differences. Conflicts and disagreements are bound to happen. If so, then how do we deal with them? If we have confidence in our capacity for reconciliation then we will be able to deal with these situations.

Anger brings us not only energy but blindness.

If you know that someone is speaking badly of you behind your back, and if you react to that negativity with a feeling of hurt, then you destroy your own peace of mind. One's pain is one's own creation. One should treat such things as if they are wind behind one's ear. In other words, just brush them aside. To a large extent, whether or not one suffers pain depends on how one responds to a given situation. What makes a difference is whether or not one is too sensitive and takes things too seriously.

When we are able to recognize and forgive ignorant actions done in one's past, we strengthen ourselves and can solve the problems of the present constructively.

Hatred is our only true enemy. Hatred has no other purpose but to destroy us. Never give it the opportunity to conquer you.

If war happens and we use all those awful weapons, there would be no victory. Both sides would suffer.

In some cases I understand certain violences that take place out of desperation. However, basically it is wrong. Violence is almost like a strong pill. It may work in one way, but the side effects may be equally strong.

Through violence you may solve one problem, but you sow the seeds for another.

Some of the greatest problems facing the world, including warfare, violence, drug abuse, and child exploitation, are caused by people not thinking about the consequences of their actions and being motivated by money.

Nonviolence is not a question of holiness, it is a question of reality.

When one is in an intense state of hatred, even a very close friend appears somehow annoying. If one harbors hateful thoughts, it ruins one's health. Even if one has wonderful possessions, in the moment of anger one feels like throwing them or breaking them. So there is no guarantee that wealth alone can give one the joy or fulfillment that one seeks.

The enemy is a very good teacher.

By internal disarmament I mean ridding ourselves of all the negative emotions that result in violence. External disarmament will also have to be done gradually, step by step.

Nonviolence means to be of service to our fellow beings.

Violence and war have always been part of human history, and in ancient times there were winners and losers. However, there would be no winners at all if another global conflict were to occur today.

Violence, once it starts, is by its nature very unpredictable. Originally you intend limited use of force. Then counter reaction. Difficult to stop. Devastation. So always, I feel, it is better to avoid.

Forgiveness is the most effective way of dealing with arguments; altruism and forgiveness bring humanity together so that no conflict, however serious, will go beyond the bounds of what is truly human.

If the love within your mind is lost and you see other beings as enemies, then no matter how much knowledge or education or material comfort you have, only suffering and confusion will ensue.

The ultimate way to solve human problems is with nonviolence.

Decisions become wrong decisions under the influence of inner armament.

It may surprise you, perhaps, but I am not strictly opposed to the spectacle of violence and crime. It all depends on the lessons you draw from it.

If the mind is dominated by hatred, the best part of the brain, which is used to judge right and wrong, does not function properly.

Don't let a little dispute injure a great friendship.

217

When a faulty deed has been done, after learning that it was wrong, one can be engaged in disclosure of the faulty deed (in presence of actual or imagined holy beings) and develop an intention not to do that action again in the future. This diminishes the force of the ill deed.

It is our enemies who provide us with the challenge we need to develop the qualities of tolerance, patience, and compassion.

Nonviolence is the only way. Even if you achieve your goal by violent means there are always side effects, and these can be worse than the problem. Violence is against human nature.

When you encounter some problems, if you point your finger at yourself and not at others, this gives you control over yourself and calmness in a situation, where otherwise self-control becomes problematic.

Ideally one should have a great deal of courage and strength, but not boast or make a big show of it. Then, in times of need, one should rise to the occasion and fight bravely for what is right.

Tolerance does not mean you just accept whatever people do. No. You have to take proper measures. You must make a distinction between the person and the action.

One thing we can do is, we can practice forgiveness, and underlying forgiveness is the ability to distinguish between the individual and the act.

For a person who cherishes compassion and love, the practice of tolerance is essential, and for that, an enemy is indispensable. So we should be grateful to our enemies, for it is they who can best help us develop a tranquil mind.

Resist when you must, but insist on achieving your aim and persist until you get it.

It is important not to have unrealistic expectations that we will find a magic key to help get rid of all suffering. It takes determination, patience, and more than one week.

Many difficulties arise from ideological or even religious conflicts, and men fight each other for means or methods, losing sight of their human ends and goals.

In order to make nonviolence, which is a physical expression of compassion, a reality, we must first work on internal disarmament and then proceed to work on external disarmament.

EMOTIONS & HEALTH

Feelings of anger, bitterness, and hate are negative. If I kept those inside me they would spoil my body and my health. They are of no use.

I like to let my thoughts come to me each morning before I get up. I meditate for a few hours and that is like recharging. After that, my daily conduct is usually driven by the motivation to help, to create a positive atmosphere for others.

In my childhood, I had a religious assistant who always told me, "If you can really laugh with full abandonment, it's very good for your health."

Some people, sweet and attractive, and strong and healthy, happen to die young. They are masters in disguise teaching us about impermanence.

This observation, that emotion and consciousness are not the same thing, tells us that we do not have to be controlled by our thoughts and emotions.

If the mind is tranquil and occupied with positive thoughts, the body will not easily fall prey to disease.

Some of you feel that you lose your independence if you don't let your mind just wander when it wants to, if you try to control it. But, that is not the case. If your mind is proceeding in the correct way, one already has the correct opinion. But if your mind is proceeding in an incorrect way, then it's necessary, definitely to exercise control.

Spirituality is like a medicine. To heal the illness, it is not sufficient to look at the medicine and talk about it: You have to ingest it.

What irritates us in the first place is that our wishes are not fulfilled. But remaining upset does nothing to help fulfill those wishes. So we neither fulfill our wishes nor regain our cheerfulness! This disconcerted state, from which anger can grow, is most dangerous. We should try never to let our happy frame of mind be disturbed. Whether we are suffering at present or have suffered in the past, there is no reason to be unhappy.

When you have fear, you can think: "Others have fear similar to this; may I take to myself all of their fears." Even though you are opening yourself to greater suffering, taking greater hardship on yourself, your fear lessens.

If you have fear of some pain or suffering, you should examine whether there is anything you can do about it. If you can, there is no need to worry about it; if you cannot do anything, then also there is no need to worry.

I think compared to other people I have not much worry.

You need some relaxation, mental as well as physical. They all converge into the same point.

The ultimate state of mind is clear light, but its clarity can be covered up by negative emotional states such as anger, hatred, or anxiety.

Whenever you find discomfort, calamities, you should know how to transport it to positive practices. It would be senseless not to see your own ill deeds as the factors that harm you.

When there is restlessness—too much hope and desire which cannot be fulfilled—this causes unhappiness and depression.

Ignorance is the fundamental cause of the painful round and round of cyclic existence.

Pleasurable sensation is a form of suffering. It plants the seed of dissatisfaction.

If you let negative emotions and thoughts arise inside you without any sense of restraint, without any mindfulness of their negativity, then in a sense you are giving them free reign. However, if you develop mindfulness of their negativity, then when they occur, you will be able to stamp them out as soon as they arise. You will not give them the opportunity or the space to develop into full-blown negative emotional thoughts.

Anger is the ultimate troublemaker. I feel you can express a strong disapproval or dislike of an object without losing your temper.

I find that there are two kinds of fear. In one kind, things are quite delicate, or critical. At such times, I know what to do or not. First, I try to consult with my friends and reflect on it. Then I make a decision and act, and I never have any regret. Ultimately, this is very much related to motivation. If I have no negative, selfish motivation, deep down I will have no guilty feeling. A second kind of fear is based on imagination. To overcome that, you need calmness so that you can investigate it more closely. When you look into it in detail, your imaginary fear dissipates.

In the Buddhist view, hatred, anger, and desire are afflictive emotions, which simply means they tend to cause us discomfort. The discomfort arises from the mental unease that follows the expression of these emotions.

Projections bring about the powerful emotional interaction between external objects and ourselves: people or things we desire. For example, when we are attracted to something, we tend to exaggerate its qualities, seeing it as one hundred percent good or one hundred percent desirable, and we are filled with a longing for that object or person.

I love smiles. That is a fact. How to develop smiles? There are a variety of smiles. Some smiles are sarcastic. Some smiles are artificial—diplomatic smiles. These smiles do not produce satisfaction, but rather fear or suspicion. But a genuine smile gives us hope, freshness.

I myself still occasionally become irritated and angry and use harsh words toward others. Then, a few moments later when the anger has subsided, I feel embarrassed; the negative words are already spoken, and there is no way to take them back. Although the words have been uttered and the sound of the voice has ceased to exist, their impact still lives on. Hence, the only thing I can do is to go to the person and apologize, isn't that right?

Anger needs to be controlled, but not hidden from yourself.

We cannot feel desire and hatred at exactly the same time toward the very same object. We can certainly have these feelings at different times, but not in the very same moment, which shows that these two attitudes function in contradiction to each other. When one of them increases in strength, the other decreases.

If distressing emotions such as anger were in the very nature of the mind, then from its inception the mind would always have to angry. Obviously, this is not so. Only under certain circumstances do we become angry.

I think in our daily experience, daily life, when we develop strong emotions, then you can't see the reality.

It is because of the intimate relationship between mind and body, and the existence of special physiological centers within our body, that physical yoga exercises and the application of special meditative techniques aimed at training the mind can have positive effects on health.

Indulgence in resentment and vengeance will only further increase miseries to oneself and others in this life and in lives to come.

Anger deceives us. Try to distance yourself from anger.

Through good times and bad times, we Tibetans try to keep our spiritual health and our good humor, remembering that all people, whether they harm us or help us, are ultimately our friends.

Normally I am in very good health. My officials and advisers have always been recommending that I relax more and take more rest.

Like the traditional Chinese and Indian systems, Tibetan medicine views health as a question of balance. A variety of circumstances such as diet, lifestyle, seasonal and mental conditions can disturb this balance.

A narrow-minded, self-centered attitude is the basis for negative emotions like fear, anxiety, and frustration.

MIND &
INSIGHT

I always keep in mind [the need to] avoid any inconvenience and embarrassment to anyone.

In Tibetan, the word for blessing means "Transformation through majesty or power." In short, the meaning blessing is to bring about, as a result of the experience, a transformation in one's mind for the better.

When you lose, don't lose the lesson.

Can the mind even see the mind? We have to answer yes and no. No, because the mind can't be a subject and object at the same time. The mind interferes, whether it wants to or not, whether it knows it or not, in all that it observes; and with all the more reason when it is a question of itself. But the mind cannot see itself completely. However, the principal toll for purifying the mind is the mind itself. The mind is its own creator, at every instant. Hence its responsibility, which is essential.

If through practice of insight you develop a sense of ease, then time has no relevance. If you're miserable, time does matter. It's so unbearable, so enormous you want to get out of it as soon as possible.

If any sensible person thinks deeply, he will respect justice. There is an inborn appreciation and respect for justice within our human body. In children, we find what is natural to be human character. But as they grow up, they develop a lot of conditioning and wrong attitudes. I often feel there is more truthfulness in a small child and I find reasons to have confidence in human courage and human nature.

If anything I've said seems useful to you, I'm glad. If not, don't worry. Just forget about it.

When you realize you have made a mistake, take immediate steps to correct it.

When a problem first arises, try to remain humble and maintain a sincere attitude, and be concerned that the outcome is fair.

To remain discouraged is not the way of a human being, we are not birds and animals, so it is not enough for us to simply lament and complain but we should use our intelligence and work hard.

If one assumes a humble attitude, one's own good qualities will increase. Whereas if one is proud, one will become jealous of others, one will look down on others, and due to that there will be unhappiness in society.

The very purpose of meditation is to discipline the mind and reduce afflictive emotions.

The training of the mind is an art. If this can be considered as art, one's life is art. I am not interested in the physical aspect of art. I simply meditate and train my mind. And as far as external appearance is concerned, nature in its pristine form is also art.

Before I sleep, if my mind is active, I calculate what I've done that is positive, what mistakes, make confession, sometimes prostrations. Around 9PM I go to sleep. Without a sleeping pill. I can go to sleep very easily, very peacefully.

If you're more relaxed, I think your brain functions more effectively. Tibetans, generally speaking, are quite jovial. In my family, we were always laughing.

A mind that is characterized by unrest will not be tranquil even in the presence of great calm.

Training the mind to think differently, through meditation, is one important way to avoid suffering and be happy.

Human intelligence should be used properly, which alone could lead to subduing physical pain and lead to a meaningful life.

Intelligence itself is the ultimate source of power.

If a problem is fixable, if a situation is such that you can do something about it, then there is no need to worry. If it's not fixable, then there is no help in worrying. There is no benefit in worrying whatsoever.

If you are too sensitive, then negative things happen. Nowadays, I realize how important it is to keep your mental state calm.

I always try to think at a deeper level, to find ways to console.

Others think of me as a healer. That is absolutely wrong. If there is a real healer, I want to see him.

A disciplined mind will help one control anger.

You need some relaxation, mental as well as physical. They all converge into the same point.

If we are very forbearing, then something we would normally consider very painful will not appear so bad after all. But without patient endurance, even the smallest thing becomes unbearable. A lot depends on our attitude.

Sometimes it's very difficult to explain why people do the things they do... You'll often find that there are no simple explanations. If we were to go into the details of individual lives, since a human being's mind is so complex, it would be quite difficult to understand what is going on, what exactly is taking place.

In this age of degeneration when one meets with all sorts of problems and adverse circumstances, the practice of generating positive thoughts is very effective. If someone lacks this practice, even though that person might be a very serious meditator, he or she will meet with many hardships and hurdles.

Our state of mind plays a major role in our day-to-day experiences as well as our physical and mental well-being. If a person has a calm and stable mind, this influences his or her attitude and behavior in relation to others. In other words, if someone remains in a peaceful and tranquil state of mind, external surroundings can cause them only a limited disturbance.

It is said that if you want to know what you were doing in the past, look at your body now; if you want to know what will happen to you in the future, look at what your mind is doing now.

Fulfilled desire may provide a sense of temporary satisfaction; however, the pleasure we experience upon acquiring a new car or home, for example, is usually short-lived. When we indulge our desires, they tend to increase in intensity and multiply in number. We become more demanding and less content, finding it more difficult to satisfy our needs.

If in a competitive society you are sincere and honest, in some circumstances, people may take advantage of you. If you let someone do so, he or she will be engaging in an unsuitable action and accumulating bad karma that will harm the person in the future. Thus it is permissible, with an altruistic motivation, to take counteraction in order to prevent the other person from having to undergo the effects of this wrong action.

You should see that all the external dirt and dust around you is basically a manifestation of the faults and stains within your mind. The most important aim is to purge these stains and faults from your mind. Therefore, as you cleanse the environment, think that you are also purifying your mind.

Guilt, as experienced in the Western culture, is connected with hopelessness and discouragement and is past-oriented. Genuine remorse, however, is a healthy state of mind—it is future-oriented, connected with hope, and causes us to act, to change.

A consciousness that conceives of inherent existence does not have a valid foundation. A wise consciousness, grounded in reality, understands that living beings and other phenomena—mind, bodies, buildings, and so forth—do not inherently exist. This is the wisdom of emptiness. Understanding reality exactly opposite to the misconception of inherent existence, wisdom gradually overcomes ignorance.

Students who become overly attached to one subject become lopsided; many subjects need to be studied.

A strong ego is needed, but without becoming egotistical. To make a wish that you become able to help all beings throughout space, you need a strong self; with a weak self such an intention is impossible.

In order to achieve a calm mind, the more you have a sense of caring for others, the deeper your satisfaction will be.

What I believe, according to my own experience, is that a calm, peaceful mind is a very important element for sustaining the body in a balanced way.

Western brains work, they work a great deal, but always in the direction of efficiency. In that way the mind puts itself at the service of the result. Like all servants, it renounces its independence. I am talking about another form of spiritual life more detached and deeper, free from the obsession of a goal to be reached. In a way, the universal invasion of technology, everywhere it goes, lessens the life of the mind.

Take your body and mind as the laboratory, engage in some thorough research on your own mental functioning, and examine the possibility of making some positive changes within yourself.

On a daily basis, you must take more care of your mind than just money, money, money!

When we apply our reason in addressing a problem, we have to be vigilant in ensuring that we remain honest, self-aware, and unbiased; the danger otherwise is that we may fall victim to self-delusion.

Gradually, having developed our minds, we generate the wish to free ourselves from samsara, as well as the altruistic intention to help others. Similarly, little by little we can discover the path of truth within ourselves with all its characteristics—seeing the nature of impermanence in objects, the nature of selflessness in phenomena and the nature of suffering in the afflictions of sentient beings. We create happiness and freedom from suffering by depending upon the path of cessation and of truth. Therefore, the Dharma is known by Buddhists as the true refuge.

To foster inner awareness, introspection, and reasoning is more efficient that meditation and prayers.

It is through listening that your mind will turn with faith and devotion, and you will be able to cultivate joy within your mind and make your mind stable. It is through listening that you will be able to cultivate wisdom and be able to remove ignorance. Therefore, it is worthwhile to engage in listening even if it costs your life. Listening is like a torch that dispels the darkness of ignorance. And if you are able to make your mental continuum wealthy through listening, no one can steal that wealth. It is supreme wealth.

To develop patience, you need someone who willfully hurts you. Such people give us real opportunities to practice tolerance. They test our inner strength in a way that even our guru cannot. Basically, patience protects us from being discouraged.

In day-to-day life, the practice of patience helps one to maintain and sustain calmness and presence of mind.

Emptiness should be understood in the context of dependent arising and it should evoke a sense of fullness, of things created by causes and conditions. We shouldn't think that self is something that is originally there and then eliminated in meditation; in fact, it is something that never existed in the first place.

It is useful to have a certain mental attitude to reduce your problems.

To be aware of a single shortcoming within oneself is more useful than to be aware of a thousand in somebody else. Rather than speaking badly about people and in ways that will produce only friction and unrest in their lives, we should practice a purer perception of them, and when we speak of others, speak of their good qualities. If you find yourself slandering anybody, first imagine that your mouth is filled with excrement. It will break you of the habit quickly enough.

Cultivating inner discipline is a time-consuming process. Having expectations of immediate results is a sign of impatience. Ironically, what the modern man wants is the best, the fastest, the easiest, and, if possible, the cheapest way.